Then & Now
Beverley

Then & Now
Beverley

Paul Gibson

TEMPUS

Frontispiece: The variety of building styles in Minster Moorgate, seen here around 1905, provide good examples of Beverley's old and new architecture. Saundby Villas, shown here on the north side of the street, were constructed around 1904, during a busy period of house construction (see page 56).

First published 2006

Tempus Publishing Limited
The Mill, Brimscombe Port,
Stroud, Gloucestershire, GL5 2QG
www.tempus-publishing.com

British Library Cataloguing in Publication Data.
A catalogue record for this book is available from the British Library.

ISBN 0 7524 4141 8

Series design and typesetting by Liz Rudderham.
Origination by Tempus Publishing Limited.
Printed in Great Britain.

Contents

Many local photographers produced views specifically for use as picture postcards in the Edwardian era. Often sold door-to-door, these invaluable images have survived in private collections, due to a collecting craze that saw millions of cards sent from one collector to another. This view taken around 1906 of Grovehill Lane was sold at William Hall Sugdon's 'library', a popular stationer and newsagent who was situated in Wednesday Market. Without these talented photographers this book would not have been possible.

Whilst the vast majority of the images used in this book are from my own collection, I must acknowledge John Bradbury, Frank Farnsworth, Bruce Grozier and the late Renton Heathcote for their kind assistance in supplying a selection of high quality old images, which compliment my own throughout the book.

This book is dedicated to the memory of my friend and fellow collector Renton Heathcote, who sadly passed away as the book was being completed.

Brief Bibliography

Allison, K.J. (Ed.); Oxford University Press; *A History of the County of York East Riding, Volume VI, the Borough and Liberties of Beverley*; 1989.

Brown, Philip; East Yorkshire Local History Society in association with Humberside Leisure Services, Beverley; *Old Beverley*; 1983.

Deans, Patricia E. and Markham, John; Alan Sutton Publishing Ltd, Stroud; *Britain in Old Photographs: Around Beverley*; 1995.

English, Barbara. Hall, Ivan. Miller Keith and Robinson, John; HMSO; Royal Commission on Historic Monuments England, Supplementary Series; 4, *Beverley, An Archaeological and Architectural Study*; 1982,

East Riding Engineering Works; *The Gordon Car* (promotional brochure); 1913.

Gibson, Paul; Kingston Press, Hull; *A Toast to the Town: a History of Beverley's Public Houses*; 2001.

Hall, Ivan and Hall, Elizabeth; Ebor Press, York; *Historic Beverley*; 1973.

Pevsner, Nikolaus and Neave, David; Penguin Books; *Buildings of England, Yorkshire: York and the East Riding*; second edition, 1995.

Sherwood, David; East Riding of Yorkshire Council Library and Information Services in association with the Local History Unit, Hull College; *Complete Streets of Beverley*; 2002.

Smith, A.H. for the English Place Name Society; Cambridge University Press; *Volume XIV - The Place Names of the East Riding of Yorkshire and York*; 1937.

Introduction

By its very nature, a 'then and now' book suggests change; a word to strike fear into the heart of the average local and architectural historian. Fortunately, Beverley has retained a surprisingly large amount of original buildings, many dating from the seventeenth and eighteenth centuries. Visitors from around the world mingle with more local travellers to wander its ancient streets, and marvel at the variety of buildings from the different periods of Beverley's history.

The first thing that struck me whilst making the modern photographs was how Beverley has changed so little, in comparison to many villages and towns, that have become overwhelmed by redevelopment. The motor car has an awful lot to answer for here; the construction of new roads to divert traffic from the town centre has done the most damage to Beverley's streetscape. The masses of parked cars have also had a detrimental effect on the street scene; almost every street in Beverley now has parked cars or double yellow lines, and the obligatory signage that goes with it. Fortunately, planning departments are now more in tune with public feeling, and aware of the value of architectural heritage, and whilst much has already been lost, there has been a great shift in opinion regarding the worth of buildings that would have been swept away in the not-too- distant past. Whilst historically only churches and more visible civic buildings had generally been given protection and funding for preservation, now a wider view is taken. When a building or road is scheduled for renovation, or where planning applications are submitted for building works, plans are scrutinised for any work that will affect diversely the character of the buildings concerned. New developments have to meet certain criteria, regarding their place in their surroundings, and how the new-builds will affect the older buildings around them. This was first given impetus by an act of 1968, which made the whole of Beverley's historic centre a conservation area; stretching from the Beck right up to North Bar Without. Groups like the Campaign for Real Ale (CAMRA) have given much needed advice and guidance to pub owners and brewing consortiums, to help protect the integrity of Beverley's many historic inns and public houses. Local civic societies and history groups campaign to save buildings of historic importance, when they are threatened with demolition or unsympathetic renovation. All in all, the picture is very positive at the present time, and long may it remain so.

In compiling this collection of old views and modern comparisons it is evident that some change is inevitable, however – due to the small physical scale of most of Beverley's commercial properties, many shops and other premises have retained their intimate character. This gives Beverley an enviable streetscape, which has remained unchanged (with some obvious exceptions) for centuries. Although the inhabitants may have changed over the years, the premises themselves have survived the onslaught of modern society and its demand for change. Modern shop fronts cannot hide the history that lies behind them; try looking above the shop frontages next time you go shopping, or for a walk around Beverley. When your eyes are tuned-in it's amazing to see the wealth of architecture surviving just above eye-level. On a positive note, it is pleasing that Beverley is still full of small shops, which all do well.

Obviously, Beverley has grown, and its increased population has caused many suburbs to develop from the mid-Victorian era onwards. In general, the standard of architecture has been very high, and Beverley's house prices bear witness to the quality of design and materials that were used in the creation of its new streets. More modern developments, from perhaps the 1930s onwards, have seen a decline in standards, but this is not peculiar to Beverley, and reflects a situation where demand outstripped supply. This was followed, post Second World War, by an austere period when a shortage of building materials meant new properties were severely restricted in terms of design.

Sadly, Beverley has also suffered from the disappointing architectural low points of the 1960s and 1970s. There is hope here however, and there is now a much-improved character to new buildings in Beverley. Recent housing developments around the Beckside area for example, are of a very high standard and have totally transformed the image of the neighbourhood. New civic buildings have on the whole been sympathetically designed and will sit well in their historic surroundings once the 'shock of the new' has receded. It is tempting to want new buildings to look old, to reflect the character of their, often ancient, neighbours. Personally, I feel this is not always a positive approach to the problem of new buildings; modern architecture should be given a chance. I think our opinion of modern building design is coloured by the bad experiences of the 1960s and 1970s, but if we put ourselves in the place of a Victorian architect – I'm sure he would have been chastised and written about in the local press, had he designed 'new' buildings in the 1890s for example, which simply copied the Georgian ones that had gone before. Resisting the forward movement of architectural design is a dangerous thing; do we really want a world where every new building is simply a clone of an old building? I think it is refreshing to see good new buildings sitting alongside more historic examples; will future generations appreciate towns full of copies, or will they want a fair representation of the current building fashions of our time?

I have chosen not to describe Beverley's history in this brief introduction as it has been well documented by historians previously; for those interested in discovering the details of Beverley's fascinating history and architecture, I would recommend the books listed in the bibliography, and a visit to the Beverley library and the East Riding Archives, as well as the many local history classes that are held by groups throughout the area. The photographs could no doubt speak for themselves, but captions are provided to assist the reader. The author has produced the new photographs, but modern cameras and lenses do not allow for an exact reproduction. The new images are for comparison and assistance in locating the original view.

1

The Markets

The view from the tower of St Mary's church, looking southeast across Beverley's ancient rooftops, has seen little change since this photograph was used as a picture postcard one hundred years ago; thankfully, the majority of these historic buildings have been preserved.

Beverley's weekly markets have been integral to its character since they began in the twelfth century. Saturday Market, as the larger market area has been known since the sixteenth century, may once have been much larger, probably extending north as far as Hengate. Over the centuries blocks of property have filled the north end of the site. Amongst these buildings is the Old Corn Exchange, seen in the top right of this photograph, which shows Saturday Market *c.* 1930. Built in 1886, the Corn Exchange replaced an earlier building, and was converted to a cinema in 1911 as it is shown here – The Picture Playhouse. Sadly the Playhouse is now closed and awaiting redevelopment, but the market goes on; the scene is now much busier than the early view, as the public are much more mobile and travel from outlying towns and cities, all that has changed is the variety of goods and the character of the vehicles.

Situated at the north end of Saturday Market, Beverley's Market Cross has changed little since it was constructed around 1711-1714 to replace an older cross, which had stood in the market since the fifteenth century. Funds for the construction came mainly from Sir Charles Hotham and Sir Michael Wharton; the eight decorative urns were placed upon the roof in 1797. These days the cross is more often the location for a band recital, or skate-boarders rather than any trading significance. The old photograph, from around 1906, was apparently taken in the early morning, and to make the same view it was necessary to get up just as early, as the market area is now given over to car parking, which dominates the area from the early morning until late evening. Happily many original shop fronts survive, but the Market Cross Coffee Tavern has now become part of a bank, and Haddlesey's Temperance Hotel, is now a craft and gift shop. Just behind the cross is Akrill's gun shop (see page 36).

Now officially known by its colloquial name, The Push Inn in Saturday Market is a popular venue for the younger drinkers in Beverley's town centre. The market place of any town or village is traditionally the location for at least one or two inns or taverns; in the case of Beverley's Saturday Market, at least seven have served the market traders and public over the last one hundred years. Shown here in the early years of the last century, The Push Inn was rebuilt around 1755 and was formerly the apothecary and spirit merchant's shop of James Mould Robinson from around 1851. At the time of the older photograph it was the premises of Mills & Sowerby, who were also wines and spirits merchants. Although the historic frontage has survived relatively intact, internally it has undergone severe alteration beginning in the 1990s. Despite its Grade II Listed Building status many irreplaceable, and historically important, fixtures and fittings were lost during the 'improvement' works.

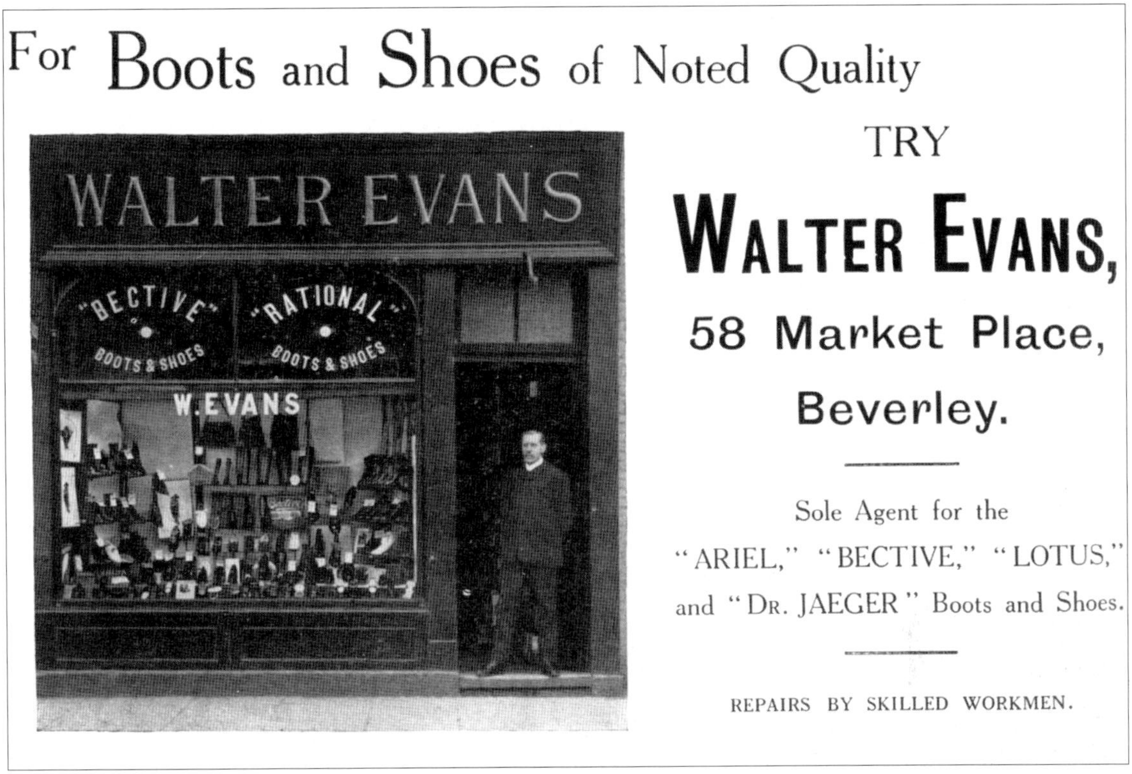

Beverley is now a very popular destination for shoppers from all around East Yorkshire, mostly due to the weekly markets, excellent facilities and friendly atmosphere of the town. Dotted around the Saturday Market are tiny shops, many of which have their origins in the eighteenth century. One such shop was the boot and shoe shop of Walter Evans on the west side of the market, almost opposite the Market Cross. William Evans had been a shoemaker in Beverley since at least 1851, and by 1855 Walter Evans is listed in trade directories as a shoemaker in the Market Place. This advertisement from around 1913 shows what must be the son of Walter senior at the door of the shop. Walter retired from business in the late 1920s and the shop eventually became a tailor's store, which it remained until at least 1967. These days it is much remodelled and forms part of the Edinburgh Woollen Mill shop; as the new picture shows, the many small shops in Beverley thrive on the trade from the market shoppers.

Beverley's markets had been held every Wednesday and Saturday since at least 1293; Wednesday Market may have been Beverley's first market, but had ceased to be used by the eighteenth century. Stalls that have been pitched there (since 1984) are simply overflow stalls from the main Saturday market.

Wednesday Market may originally have been much larger, forming a large triangle stretching from the north side of the Minster, with Eastgate and Highgate as its boundaries. In the same way as Saturday Market, it is likely to have been built upon by the thirteenth century, leaving the familiar small triangle we know now.

This old view of around 1908 shows the east side of Wednesday Market, with the boot factory of John Musson (far left) now Figaro's gift shop; the original Queen's Head pub (rebuilt in 1926); Tanfield's cycle shop and Hardy's fruit shop, now merged as Peck's speciality food store; a private house, now a chiropractor's and curry house; Sugden's stationers, and a chemist at the corner, now form a furniture shop.

The location of this quaint corner pub can be seen on page 14, at the junction of Eastgate and Wednesday Market. The Railway Tavern was housed within a seventeenth century building and had been a pub since at least 1846; it first appeared in trade directories that year, the same year that Railway Street was opened directly east of the building. Railway Street linked Wednesday Market with the new railway station.

The small pub was owned by T. Linsley & Co. Ltd of Hull and closed in 1918, when £1,400 was paid to the brewery in compensation. The building remained empty until around 1924 when it was demolished for the widening of the narrow junction of Eastgate.

Looking at the empty plot that the pub stood on it is difficult to see how it fitted, but it must be borne in mind that the plot was reduced in size during the road widening.

Wednesday Market has had at least four pubs in the last 200 years; The French Horn (see page 15), The Spotted Cow, which is now Ye Old Pork Shoppe, a butcher; The Queen's Head (see page 14) and of course – The Railway Tavern. Now only The Queen's Head survives as a pub, although several cafes in the market have drinks' licences; the dwindling number of pubs can be seen as a sign of changing tastes, with many people choosing to either drink at home or choosing to dine-out in our more affluent society.

The huge chapel shown here dominated the west side of Wednesday Market from its construction in 1867 (see date on building) on the site of an older chapel, school (behind) and shops. Built for the Primitive Methodist Connexion, the new chapel had seating for 800; almost double that of the original chapel, and a much larger Sunday school at the rear. As attendance in churches diminished throughout the country, chapels like this became redundant. The Wednesday Market chapel was demolished in 1958-59 and replaced by Crystal Motor Garage, which survived into the 1980s, and from around 1994 by Boyes Ltd, which it remains.

Just north of the chapel, shown to the left of the two pictures on page 17, was the Spotted Cow, a beerhouse held by Benjamin Ramshaw at the time of this photograph taken around 1920. The Spotted Cow also served as a butcher's shop and, almost 170 years after its first record in the trade directories, it remains a butcher's, known as The Olde Pork Shoppe and is now a listed building.

G JACK & SON LTD
Speciality Foods
SOLD
BOYES
MAN

WORTHINGTONS ALES
QUEEN'S HEAD
ALES
CYCLE STORE

These views contrast the changing face of the west side of Wednesday Market; the early view of around 1906 shows a tranquil early morning scene looking south into Highgate towards the Minster. The shop of D.H. Witty, printer and stationer, on the far right of the older picture, stood next to a grand five-bay property known as Highgate House, latterly occupied by Mrs W. Bolton, but derelict by the time of this postcard view.

The house had probably been vacated in readiness for the construction of Lord Roberts Road, which took place in 1909 (see page 92), and cut through the house to form a link from Wednesday Market to Well Lane, thus creating a route west to Lairgate. The 2006 photograph shows the house reduced to three bays, now a solicitor's office.

To the left of the pictures can be seen a building with a seventeenth-century core, possibly a former inn known as The French Horn. This was latterly a cafe, but is now another gift shop serving Beverley's many tourists.

2

Between the Markets

A peaceful afternoon around 1905, looking north into Butcher Row, and the junction with Walkergate. The granite-set street has now been pedestrianised and the shops have changed, but the scene is otherwise quite similar.

Toll Gavel is one of Beverley's more unusual street names, and formed part of the original long High Street, or 'Alta Via', although the origin of the name is uncertain. Recorded as 'Tole Gavell', and from the fourteenth century as 'Toll Gavell'. Gavell is an historic family name and although not well known in this area, it is possible that tolls were collected by, or for, the Gavel family here. Pavage tolls had been charged in Beverley, to raise funds for the paving of streets, as early as the year 1255.

Shown here looking north towards Saturday Market around 1904, Toll Gavel continues to form the backbone of Beverley's shopping area, and has managed to retain much of its character. To the right of the older picture can be seen the hanging sign of a Golden Ball, outside the former pub of the same name. To the rear of the pub was Stephenson's Golden Ball Brewery, demolished by Woolworth in 1969 following their purchase of the property. Toll Gavel was pedestrianised in 1982.

This view looks south, from the same point as the photograph on page 20, into the evocatively titled Butcher Row; a name that has been used for the route between Wednesday Market and Toll Gavel, since the eighteenth century. Originally forming part of one long High Street, it had been known as Fish Market Gate in the thirteenth century, and was the site of a regular fish market. At that time the name Butcher Row had also been used for part of Hengate, North Bar Within and the north side of Saturday Market; most likely a name that followed the location of the butchers' stalls, as they relocated around the town from one century to the next.

Sadly, the early years of this century saw the last butcher in Butcher Row shut up shop as more supermarkets invaded Beverley and convenience shopping came to the historic market town. To the left of this photograph taken around 1910 can be seen the offices of one of Beverley's old newspapers, *The Independent*, which ran from 1888 until 1911.

Running north from Cross Street is Register Square, shown here around 1906; Cross Street was previously named Register Street. Having had several earlier names, the present Register Square has been used since around 1708, possibly because the East Riding Registry of Deeds was established in Beverley in 1707, or, because it led to the home of the registrar, whose house was situated at its end.

To the right of the picture is the present post office, built on a former garden plot in 1905 to replace an earlier office of around 1852 that stood opposite. Although the scene appears unchanged, note that the ground floor of the post office is completely altered, and the grand door case gone.

The classical building in the background is the Guildhall, with its 1835 portico designed by Charles Mountain junior. The frontage hides a much earlier fifteenth-century building, from which some original timber-framed walls were uncovered in the early 1980s.

The Baptist chapel, mentioned in the title of this postcard view of around 1905, is the large building at the end of the street. This was the Well Lane Baptist chapel, and Well Lane ran left to right across the picture, just in front of the building. The street in the foreground, running towards the chapel, is Cross Street. The chapel was demolished for the construction of Lord Roberts Road in 1909 (see page 92), and is now the site of a mini-roundabout. This opened out Cross Street, as we see it today. The building on the left is Lansdowne House, built around 1834, by Edward Page, and still a private residence. The railings on the right are protecting the former 'Constitution House', a Victorian gentleman's club built around 1830; this was later the County Records Office and still forms part of the East Riding Archives offices.

The historic nature of Toll Gavel and Butcher Row was well illustrated by this humble row of buildings, shown here around 1905. Nos 33 to 39 Butcher Row, situated at its south-east side, were timber-framed and dated from the seventeenth century. The arched entry led to Brigham's Yard, named by owner George Brigham, a cabinet maker.

The small court contained eight tiny dwellings with four privies; in contrast, beyond the dwellings was a large garden and private house facing Wilbert Lane.

The houses were demolished around 1912 for the Marble Arch cinema, which was built on the site in 1916, taking its name from the arched entry, often referred to as Marble Arch.

As audiences fell, the cinema too was demolished just fifty years later in 1967; the demolition also included a famous Beverley shop, that of Greswell's home furnishings and antiques store. The site is now occupied by one of Beverley's first supermarkets, marking a distinct change in the appearance of Beverley's street line, and the inevitable change in shopping methods.

On 24 July, 1912, at around 2 p.m., a dramatic cloudburst occurred over Beverley that was to push Beverley's ancient drainage systems past their limit. Rainwater flooded down from the Westwood and ran through the Willow Grove neighbourhood into the centre of town. The low-lying area around Walkergate suffered badly as this photograph shows. Ancient watercourses criss-cross Beverley, now mostly culverted; one, known as Walker Beck, ran close to Walkergate on its journey south under Minster Moorgate and the fields beyond. The extreme conditions caused this to overflow and flood the area.

Looking into Walkergate from the junction of Butcher Row and Toll Gavel, the children paddle past the yard of builder George Pape, whose yard had a footpath leading to his other premises in Reindeer Yard, off Wilbert Lane; a chemist shop now marks the site. To the left of picture, the old bay window has gone, now the rear of an outdoor clothing shop, which no doubt sells Wellingtons and wet-weather gear!

Another victim of the 1912 flooding was Well Lane, which runs south from Butcher Row to the junction with Lord Roberts Road. This view, looking west down Well Lane, shows the typical small houses that are common in Beverley.

The name Well Lane is self explanatory, as there were two wells in the lane at one time. Prior to the construction of Lord Roberts Road in 1909, Well Lane ran all the way to Lairgate, and during the fifteenth century was known as Fish Market Moorgate or Market Moorgate. The term gate is taken from the ancient word 'gata' meaning 'the way across', often used for road names, hence Moorgate – literally the road or way to the moors. Fish Market Moorgate would translate to the way from the fish market (an ancient name for Butcher Row) to the moors.

Well Lane now only has nine surviving original buildings, although it is still a residential area; the site of many the tiny terraced houses is now taken up with modern flats, car parking, and small business premises.

3

Shopping

This impressive shop front is that of grocer and provisions merchant Richard Care, situated in Saturday Market, the first property beyond the end of Toll Gavel. Richard Care was born in Tickton near Beverley, and the 1901 Census records him living above his premises, with his wife, a son and two daughters; a servant also lived in. He had been in business in Beverley since the late 1880s, at Nos 40-41 Market Place, as shown in the photograph. He extended his business around 1898, with an extra shop at Nos 41-43 Eastgate, near the corner of Chantry Lane. Although the Care's larger shop survived well into the 1950s, it's a sad fact that most stores of this kind were forced out by the gradual encroachment of supermarkets from the late 1950s onwards. It is rare to see such an interesting window display these days as supermarkets have little or no need to display their wares to attract trade. I would suggest that a display like this was more about pride, than simple economics.

DENT'S
GLOVES

The two older photographs show three generations of the Nicholls family. The oldest photograph opposite dates from the late 1890s and shows spinsters, Anne Nicholls (centre) and her sister Emma (right), with their niece Emma (left), outside No. 2 North Bar Within.

The shop had been in the family since around 1870; thirty-six-year-old Emma Nicholls was recorded as a glover and hosier at the shop in the 1871 census, with her sister Jane and young niece Anne E., who was just seven. By the time of the 1901 census Ann E., by then a spinster, was thirty-seven and head of house, with her sister Emma, thirty, and niece, also Emma, fourteen. The sisters were recorded as 'stay makers and fancy dealers', resident above the shop. An elderly Miss Anne Nicholls can be seen in the second photograph (left) from the 1930s. The sisters were still listed at the shop in a 1939 trade directory. The shop is relatively unchanged and now a shoe shop.

Most people would presume that fish and chip shops are a relatively new phenomenon, however they were first introduced to the north of England in the early 1860s. Fried fish shops had been around longer, and potatoes had been fried since the early eighteenth century, but 'chipped' potatoes were unknown until we borrowed the idea from the French in the 1860s; it was at this point that we joined the two in the 'great British meal'.

Beverley's earliest fried fish dealers appear in the early 1890s when John Andrews had a shop in Wednesday Market, and William Donaldson had a shop in Eastgate. By 1899 there were four fried fish dealers in Beverley, one being in Ladygate, possibly the shop shown here in the occupation of Harry Dale around 1910. Harry remained at his Fish and Chip Saloon, at Nos 35-37 Ladygate, for only a short while, and was gone by 1920. Signs show that he also sold meat pies for two pence and aerated water, ginger beer and hop bitter supplied by Straker's of Beverley.

The shop, No. 35 Ladygate, was demolished along with many other architecturally important buildings in the street in 1980. The architects of the bland buildings that now occupy the site (an amusement hall with cafe) have shown little regard for the timber-framed, late-medieval houses that they have replaced. The modern photograph also shows the rebuilt Dog and Duck pub, to the far left of the picture, built on the site of the original eighteenth-century pub that was demolished in 1929.

To the left, or north of Harry Dale's fish and chip saloon, shown in the last photograph, can be seen a small part of the Dog and Duck Inn. Situated at the corner of Dog and Duck Lane, now named after the pub but historically known as Shoemaker Lane and later Burdett Lane, the pub dates back to the eighteenth century although the present building is of 1929. Doubtless thousands of Beverley's shoppers have stopped off at the Dog and Duck over the years for a pub lunch or a swift half.The present manager is Mark McMullen, whose family have held the pub for over thirty years; he is shown here outside the pub, which provides bed and breakfast and excellent bar meals.

Former landlord Ted Andrews is shown here around 1910, with a firm grip on his trusty terrier, alongside what was hopefully a stuffed duck; no doubt today our strict restrictions on hygiene and cleanliness would render such a scene unacceptable. It is pleasing to note however, that most of Beverley's pubs do remain 'dog friendly', thankfully a tradition that most Beverlonians appreciate.

It is likely to be Mrs Rhoda Hunsley standing at the door of her shop, which was situated at No. 24 Norwood. The Hunsley family were prominent in the Norwood area, and Hunsley's Yard stood just to the west of the shop, between the yard and Rhoda's shop were two other family businesses – that of Thomas, a joiner, and John, a cow keeper. The yard was named after Thomas Hunsley senior, a wheelwright, who was established there by around 1860. The window shows that Rhoda sold a variety of goods, including cakes, sweets and meats, possibly from the family cow-keeping business. She was listed in the trade directories from the 1890s as a pork butcher, and remained in business until the early 1930s. In 1931 Rhoda would have been seventy years old; the business carried on in the hands of her daughter Florence until around 1938.

At the time of this photograph of around 1910, there were at least thirty-six butchers in Beverley, but by 1967 there were only thirteen, the effect of supermarkets having begun to take their toll on the small shops. Sadly, No. 24 Norwood was demolished, probably for the construction of the supermarket located to the rear of Norwood, and whose entrance runs directly over the site of the old shop. See also, pages 65 and 66.

Charles Edwin Stephenson's fine window display contained many picture postcards of the town, some of which have no doubt been used to compile this book. Shown here around 1915, it shows a wide diversity of items that he supplied under the heading of 'art stationer', dealing also in 'leather and fancy goods'. The craze for collecting picture postcards of an area had reached a peak in 1905, and tens of millions of postcards were sent daily to addresses throughout England. Collectors would often send cards in envelopes so as not to spoil the card, although some just sent them in the normal way, unwittingly providing a valuable dating tool for future historians; the postmark will give a latest possible date for the photograph on the card.

Charles had been in business since the late 1890s at this shop, with the prominent address of No. 1 North Bar Within. He was one of only half a dozen stationers in the town at that time.

Mrs Stephenson was listed as the proprietor by 1936, and in 1937 William Carpenter Fifield took over, retaining the trade as a bookseller and stationer.

He remained only two years, and Ralph Lester took over in 1939, continuing a long succession of changes in management. However, the shop remains, still a newsagent in 2006, over a hundred years later, and now known as North Bar News, happily retaining the fine Victorian shop frontage.

From the late 1890s, until at least 1910, No .4 Toll Gavel was home to draper and milliner Frank Hanlay-Robinson. Originally from Otley, it is Frank standing in the doorway with his wife and daughters. When Frank opened shop there were at least twenty-two other milliners and drapers in Beverley in direct competition with his relatively modest shop on the west side of Toll Gavel; six of those were also situated in Toll Gavel, and one was directly opposite the Hanlay-Robinson's. Many of his competitors also used large advertisements in the press, and local trade directories, whereas Frank seemed not to have been able to afford to do so, and appears to have left the trade after quite a short time in business.

Toll Gavel has surviving, original buildings, dating from as early as the seventeenth century; the Hanlay-Robinson's shop was probably a Georgian building, but was sadly demolished in recent years. The replacement buildings are remarkably plain, and show little thought for the buildings that surround them; thankfully, some of the more recent developments in Beverley have shown more taste in their design. The site of the Hanlay-Robinson's shop was rebuilt in the 1950s, the site of the former shop now forms half of a clothing shop known as M. & Co.

Percy Whiting's Tea and Coffee Emporium, at No. 5 North Bar Within, had passed from his father William, and his grandfather Thomas before him. The family had been grocers in this shop since the 1840s, and remained until the First World War. This photograph taken around 1913 shows that the shop also had a cafe, known as The Mikado Cafe.

Beverley was indeed a town of small shopkeepers, and happily it still is; latterly the former cafe has been used by a variety of trades, and the front rooms are now used by Hawley's Antiques and the Beverley offices of *The Hull Daily Mail*. Sadly the ornate frontage is hard to discern from the modern appearance of the shop, and the cafe above is now vacant.

Esau Akrill opened his shop at No.18 Saturday Market around 1828 and soon established a successful gun-making business. His sons Henry and Esau junior succeeded him from 1868 onwards and maintained the high standards of weapons, supplying them to gentry and nobility throughout England; Akrill's also had a store in Hull for some years, at No. 25 Blackfriargate (around 1848 to 1851). The firm continued to trade into the twentieth and twenty-first centuries, becoming a limited company in 1975; sadly the last gunsmith's in Beverley closed in the autumn of 2001 and the shop lay empty for some months. Now it has a new lease of life as a cafe and wine bar called Mozart's, where shoppers can sit outside and watch the world go by. The elegant bow windows, once filled with rifles, shotguns and cycle parts, now have a very different aspect as Beverley follows the national trend for cafe culture and wine bars.

4

Around the Westwood

The floods of 1912 put a stop to the usual promenading and games on the Westwood, but not for some. These intrepid sightseers couldn't resist having a look at the flooded pastures just to the west of Willow Grove.

The anonymous cottage shown in this photograph taken around 1905 marks the entrance to the Westwood from North Bar Within, and was one of many provided for those responsible for the security of the cattle and other animals that had grazing rights on the Westwood. Marked as 'Neatherd's Cottage' on the 1853 Ordnance Survey plans of the area, 'neatherd' is an ancient name for 'one who has care of cattle', and a pinfold was situated directly opposite. Several cottages were provided, situated near each gate onto the pastures, and most were rebuilt around 1856 in this Gothic style.

This road has become known as York Road, as it joins part of a network of older roads, used as a route to York for centuries. To the right, beyond the cottage and gates can be seen York Terrace, another now very desirable terrace of fine houses, many built by M.L. Whitton (see page 36) from around 1871.

One of the less-altered views in Beverley is the view west across Willow Grove, towards the open pastures, which remains as peaceful today as it was a hundred years ago. The houses are built on the line of an old pool, or dike, known as Willow Row, still shown on the 1853/54 Ordnance Survey plans of the area; this was fed by springs and the area was known by many names, e.g. Willow Springs or Willowes Well. The Westwood was once a huge woodland area, consisting mostly of oak and willow trees; hence the many willow references in this area, and it seems most likely that Willow Grove took its name from the ancient watercourse Willow Row.

Construction of the houses commenced around 1853, initially just eight houses by local builder Marmaduke Lowson Whitton, of North Bar Without; the houses were almost certainly designed by his architect brother, James Whitton of Lincoln. The terrace was extended west, in two sections some years later, the first inhabited from around 1857, according to deeds.

Nineteenth-century antiquarians discovered the remains of ancient buildings in fields behind Westwood and Albert Terraces. These have since been attributed to a Franciscan friary dating from the thirteenth century, and linked with these were agricultural areas known as St Giles' Crofts. A croft is a small piece of enclosed land, and the 'ridge and furrow' of this land is still visible in nearby school fields and gardens. This area was still named as St Giles' Crofts on the Ordnance Survey plans of 1853/54, and its rich history was reflected in the naming of a new suburban terrace looking south across the lands.

St Giles' Croft was begun in the 1860s but mostly developed during the 1870s by J.R. Blythe, and builders such as Thomas Rippon.

When first built, the houses enjoyed open views across this south-east portion of the Westwood, but now face modern housing of the late 1920s, which show a distinct decline in building standards during the first half of the twentieth century.

A number of streets with grand houses were formed on the eastern side of the Westwood as Beverley expanded during the eighteenth and nineteenth centuries; Westwood Road, Woodlands, etc., were all built on existing lanes that had led west from the town for centuries. Situated at the western end of Woodlands (see page 82) is the former Union Workhouse, shown here around 1906, facing the Westwood. It was built in 1860/61 to the designs of J.B. and W. Atkinson of York, in a mixture of Tudor and Jacobean styles, replacing an older institution in Minster Moorgate. An infirmary, casual wards, entrance arch and lodge were added in 1893/95, and it became the Westwood Hospital in 1939. Over the years many more new buildings have been added, and the former Westwood House on its north side has also been taken over. Sadly, as the new photograph shows, the character of the original building has been all but erased.

The line of Westwood Road marks part of an old network of lanes linking Howden via North and South Cave, and Walkington, with the heart of Beverley's market area. This ancient trading route led from the market area via Newbegin and through the Newbegin Bar, from which began Newbegin Lane (now Westwood Road) and across the Westwood via Cave Road (shown on Hick's plan of Beverley in 1811). Westwood Road was recorded as Newbegin Lane as early as 1329, becoming Westwood Lane as it became built-up from the 1820s. The first properties were built on the south side, and were quite humble, but as the larger houses were built along the north side from around 1850 it became Westwood Road.

Today Westwood Road is a very desirable residence, with houses fetching enormous prices; happily both sides of the street remain virtually intact with a wonderful selection of house styles. Inevitably the street's appearance is marred by the omnipresent motor car, traffic signs and yellow lines.

We are fortunate enough to have surviving remains of several old windmills in our area. Beverley Westwood had at least five well-documented mills, with remains of two surviving to this day; the lower portion of Black Mill, also known as Westwood Far Mill, or Baitson's Mill, had its origins in the early eighteenth century, and now stands alone next to the site of Beverley's old cricket ground.

The second survivor is the Union Mill, or Anti Mill as it was sometimes known; built around 1799, it was worked as a co-operative in direct competition with private mills. It fell into disuse in the 1890s and was dismantled, but the lower section survives and is now incorporated into the clubhouse of the Beverley and East Riding Golf Club, formed in 1889. Their original pavilion was near the Black Mill, but moved to this site in 1906, which is the date of this photograph. It is hard to imagine these giants in full-sail towering over the landscape.

Horse racing began on the Westwood around 1690, and has continued largely uninterrupted ever since. A grandstand was erected in 1767, and replaced in 1887, but this was later demolished. The Beverley & East Riding Race Co. Ltd was formed in 1902, and gave permission for the course to be used as an airfield during the First World War, following which racing commenced once more in 1920.

This photograph dating to around 1920 shows the very sparse stand, with just planks for the punters to stand on; compare this with the luxurious facilities shown in the modern view. The present stands were built in 1959 and 1967, with various alterations and improvements since.

Races now take place over about fifteen days each year, much more than the original races, and Beverley is packed to capacity on race days, just as it was on race days in the last two centuries. Local innkeepers would pay for the privilege of having booths on the grounds, whereas modern-day punters have indoor bar and restaurant facilities.

5

Ancient Routes

The gateway shown in this photographic postcard of around 1910, is situated within the precinct wall of a former Dominican Friary, on one of Beverley's oldest streets, Friary Lane.

To the right of this image can be seen the gateway shown on the previous page; one of several that led to a Dominican Friary, established here, *c.* 1240. The surviving building includes details from the fourteenth century, although a large part of the original site is lost beneath the railway lines to the east, and lands beyond. The buildings have only survived due to a continued effort, essentially by the general public, to save them. Armstrong Patents, who took over the site in 1960, applied to demolish the friary in 1962. Today, this pleasant street, named Friars Lane, has been complemented by a sympathetic housing development to the north and west, which does not detract from the architecturally important site that it overlooks. Few original buildings survive in the street, which once extended further east, but was divided when the railway was constructed in 1846; the eastern section is now known as Chantry Lane. The friary buildings have been used as a youth hostel since 1984.

By the end of the thirteenth century an ancient watercourse had become the main trading route into Beverley. Known simply as the Beck, and later Beverley Beck, its development is ascribed to Archbishop Thurstan, who organized its canalization during the twelfth century.

Beckside was the site of many inns and taverns, sadly none of which survive, except the rebuilt and much altered Forester's Arms; the many workers from the Beckside factories and yards ensured good trade for a number of inns. This photograph taken around 1906 shows the Beck looking east towards the town. To the left is Canal Wharf and the Top Warehouses, mostly used by coal merchants; the chimney is connected with a seed-crushing mill established in the eighteenth century, and the small building to the immediate left is a former Toll House, where river traffic paid tolls for use of the Beck.

Only a handful of original buildings survive on the right of the picture, with much new housing bringing life back into the area.

Flemingate, once a calm eastern suburb of Beverley, is now a main traffic route into the town, which suffers badly from huge numbers of vehicles at all times of day. An ancient, winding road, it was never intended to carry the large vehicles that are allowed to use it. Flemingate is first mentioned by name in the early thirteenth century, taking its name from the many Flemish merchants who established their weaving businesses there. As one of Beverley's oldest streets, Flemingate contains many ancient dwellings, such as No. 58 Flemingate, built in the artisan Mannerist style, shown to the right of these pictures; this dates from around 1660-1670 and is a remarkable survivor, situated so close to the heavy traffic. Sadly, the typical seventeenth-century Yorkshire cottages beyond No. 58 have been demolished; the Victorian buildings beyond them show how property has gradually been set back from the road. Fortunately, many Georgian buildings survive, including those shown on the left of the picture and Flemingate remains mostly private housing.

F lemingate leads into Eastgate at a busy junction where traffic from Keldgate waits to turn left or right; as this photograph taken around 1900 shows, this was not always the case.

On the left are a series of timber-framed buildings, which dated from the sixteenth century; they were demolished in 1912, when the narrow entry to Minster Yard South was opened up and the Minster wall moved back. Constitution Hall was built on the site, but it too was later demolished for the modern housing that occupies the site today. On the right, just visible, is the hanging sign of The Sun Inn, a contender for the title of the 'oldest pub in Beverley'. To the far right the small, single-storey buildings were typical examples of Beverley cottages, dating from the eighteenth century; these were demolished some years after this photograph and the present shops built upon the site. Note the small gardens of the houses on the left were also lost for the widening of Flemingate.

Highgate formed part of Beverley's High Street (first recorded as Alta Via); this was an ancient term, used for the whole of the route leading north from the Minster, all the way to the North Bar. The short section we now call Highgate formed part of this, and was also known as Londoners Street during the seventeenth century, as traders from London often rented shops there. The modern term Highgate has only been in constant use since the late seventeenth century.

The older of these two views shows Highgate looking north around 1910; to the right of the picture, with two workers standing at the gates, can be seen the carriage works of E.W. and G. Osgerby, who had been coachbuilders in Highgate since around 1870. Unusually, the frontage of their premises was clad in wooden boards. Their extensive yard and works were demolished and modern flats and shops built around 1969 fill the site, however, the site of their carriage entry remains as the entrance to the car parking from the flats.

Just out of view, in the far distance of the previous photograph, was this timber-framed building dating from the fifteenth century; its jettied appearance, with overhanging first floor, very similar to more familiar buildings in York. Situated on the west side of Highgate, just south of Wednesday Market, the building had been slightly altered, with the addition of a late-Victorian first floor shop window, but retained many important architectural details. Carved tracery window details around the first floor window, and a moulded and carved cornice separating the floors, were unique in Beverley. In what can only be described as an act of vandalism, the authorities allowed its demolition in 1956, in suspiciously swift circumstances. The speed in which it was dispatched did not allow for any adequate record of the building to be made or for the salvage of any of its unique details. The scene in 2006 is shown in the second photograph, which shows the site of the ancient building has been filled with rather ordinary housing, which has done little to fit in with its surroundings.

This needless loss should have served as a poignant reminder to the local council, however, the demolition of such important buildings continued into the 1970s and on some occasions after.

Nevertheless Highgate remains an attractive street with mostly residential housing, coffee shops and a good pub, the Monk's Walk, where locals and tourists mingle to enjoy a good lunch and a pint.

This photograph was used as a postcard, posted in 1904, and appears to show a wedding party. It may well be the bride leaving her home on the north side of Keldgate, just past the narrow junction with Lairgate. To the left of the picture is the entrance to Hoggard's Yard, earlier known as Cook's Yard, after shoemaker Joseph Cook, whose double-fronted house can be seen to the right of the entry. At the time of this photograph it was the home of cow-keeper John Hoggard, and had taken his name.

Acres of poor quality housing were crammed into yards, by owners keen to capitalise on their property; this is a stark contrast with the scene in Keldgate today, where a much more open feel prevails. The junction of Lairgate is now widened and little original property remains except that in the distance near the site of the old Tanner's Arms. Keldgate has no pubs now, the last – the Beehive, having just been demolished for housing.

The small group of uniformed personnel, seen here around 1910 were marching eastwards along Keldgate towards the location of the last image. It is likely that they had marched from the Victoria Barracks on the north side of Queensgate (see page 90) and were heading for the town centre or the Minster. To the extreme right is the end of a short terrace of five houses, which appear quite modern although they were constructed in the late 1890s. Beyond the terrace is the former Keldgate Reading Rooms, opened in the 1890s. Sadly, all of the buildings and the large wall of Lairgate Hall beyond the modern looking terrace have been lost, from the 1920s redevelopment of the area onwards. The modern photograph shows that housing has filled the site, retaining the mostly residential feel of the area, but the towering old trees shown in the old image were lost with the 1920s development of Lairgate Hall's extensive grounds.

The eastern end of Keldgate is shown here, in a photograph of around 1905; a little further on is where it meets Minster Yard South. Keldgate takes its name from the old word 'kelda', usually taken to mean a spring, hence Keld Gate – the road to a spring or well; the accounts of the keeper of the Keldgate Bar for the year 1450, reveal that a spring was located just outside the bar. Keldgate had also been known as South-Bar Gate around 1250, as it led west to one of Beverley's ancient town gates, but was affirmed as Keldgate by 1274.

Keldgate's rural nature has been all but lost, due to Beverley's continuing struggle with heavy traffic levels, although a relief road is planned. However, many of its original buildings survive, including the eighteenth-century houses shown to the left of the pictures.

The 1901 census reveals that tanning employed more people in Beverley than any other industry. Keldgate had been home to at least four tanneries, including that of George Cussons, acquired around 1834 and remaining in the family until around 1910. The site was later used by Melrose Tanners Ltd, which was the last surviving tannery in Beverley, closing in 1986. With now little or no demand for industrial sites in the area, the former tannery site was used for a housing development around 1989, and is known as Melrose Park.

Running parallel with Keldgate, to its north, is Minster Moorgate, the street's descriptive name suggesting its original purpose; that of a direct route from the ancient Minster to the moors or west woods. The street is recorded as early as the thirteenth century, and has also been referred as South Moorgate and Kirk Moorgate. The street has buildings from a variety of periods, the oldest dating to the seventeenth century, and many good examples from the eighteenth century; it was also the site of several seventeenth- and eighteenth-century 'hospitals', or almshouses (see page 56).

To the right of this photograph taken around 1905 is the former infants' school of 1888, now used for private housing; around it, on the south side of the street are good mid-eighteenth century houses.

In contrast, the new photograph shows how modern developments have been fitted in where older property has been demolished at the south-east side.

Generally, Minster Moorgate survives intact; to the far west, Minster Moorgate was extended into the imaginatively titled 'Minster Moorgate West', part of a large development in this area around 1927, when the Admiral Walker Estate was built around the new Admiral Walker Road; all of which was constructed on the former grounds of Lairgate Hall (of 1760), purchased by the council in 1926.

Minster Moorgate was the site of some of Beverley's oldest institutions, due to its close proximity to the Minster, of which Charles Wharton's Hospital (of 1689) is the only survivor. Another former almshouse is shown here, this was the Thwaite Fox Hospital established in 1639. The small cottages were adapted as a charity home for four poor widows; these were sold in 1872, but still listed in a directory of 1899 as 'three small houses', and in the 1901 Census. The ancient houses were sadly demolished in July 1904 for the construction of Saundby Villas.

Other important buildings in Minster Moorgate were a workhouse, built around 1726, and Sir Michael Wharton's almshouses, all now demolished.

The need for housing overcame any desire to protect Beverley's heritage, as the buildings were mostly privately owned, and the housing that now stands in their place is fairly standard of the Victorian and Edwardian eras. Once again, the lack of garage space causes the pretty street to be clogged-up with parked cars.

North Bar Within, seen here looking south towards the market, is remarkably unchanged, considering it is one of the main ways into, and out of, the town centre. The name is self-explanatory and literally means the road within the North Bar, the last surviving gate, which formed part of Beverley's ancient town defences.

Other than the modern fad for painting brickwork, the only noticeable change is the inevitable encroachment of car parking. Fortunately, this area is particularly wide as for many years it was a market area; during the seventeenth and eighteenth century cattle, but more often horse fairs were held here and outside the bar. This began a long link with horses in this area; the racecourse nearby provided another link, and the present Royal Standard pub was originally known as the Turf Inn, in recognition of its racing clientele.

The historic properties within the North Bar have now been converted for use as shops, restaurants and quality apartments, following a trend seen throughout the town.

Timber-framed buildings such as this one in North Bar Within are very rare, many having been demolished due to a lack of education and awareness as to their architectural importance.

Situated on the west side of North Bar Within, at the corner of Tiger Lane, No. 49 North Bar Within is shown here around 1910. Its age is self-evident, as displayed by the incredible oak timbers used for its structure; the heavy timbers would have been in-filled with wattle and daub, (a mixture of mud-clay and straw forced in by hand around panels of willow osiers). This was the style when it was built in the fifteenth century, but during the eighteenth and nineteenth centuries this mixture was replaced with local brick. This style of replacement can also be seen on the frontage of the Sun Inn, Flemingate.

No. 49 has had a varied history; the East Riding Engineering Works of engineer Gordon Armstrong was established here around 1907, with workshops at the rear of the building where he manufactured his famous Gordon car (see page 74). The property had lain partly empty for some time prior, its structure divided in two by a central passage leading to Harrison's Yard; the site of the yard was later used by Armstrong for his works, and remained in use as a garage until around 1980. Latterly, it has been divided into a series of shop units forming an arcade known as St Mary's Court.

This is a very early view of the famous Beverley Arms, taken around 1870; the pub was established by the seventeenth century, although the present building probably dates to around 1794 when it changed name from The Blue Bell Inn to The Beverley Arms.

The Westerby family, whose shop can be seen to the extreme right of picture, were coopers and basket makers, and continued in business until around 1910; their shop is now the site of a Chinese restaurant. The shop to the extreme left of picture, was demolished by Trust House Forte, who had first acquired the hotel in 1938. In 1966 they began major alterations, extending the hotel by three bays, over the site of the shop to create the present large-arched entrance. These days the hotel is still well used for weddings and functions continuing a tradition in business dating back over 300 years.

During the Middle Ages Beverley was protected by a system of ditches, earthen banks and 'bars' across the main routes into the town. The North Bar is the earliest mentioned, having been recorded in the twelfth century as *aquilo barra*. There were three other main gates or bars, fortified in the same manner as the North Bar, situated at Norwood, Newbegin, Keldgate. North Bar, shown here around 1905, was rebuilt as it appears today, in the late 1400s at a cost of one hundred pounds. Tolls were collected at the bar, for pavage amongst other things, which was used for the maintenance of the roads. During the seventeenth century the gates were locked at night, but generally the town's defences were feeble and offered little protection from marauders despite constant maintenance.

The only effective part of the defences appears to have been the town ditch, which ran outside the bar; by the eighteenth century the ditch had become a nuisance and was gradually filled-in or culverted, with the last section being filled-in in the 1930s. As the recent photograph shows, the gates are rarely shut these days; exceptions are usually ceremonial occasions, when the gates are shut and opened to admit honoured citizens given the freedom of the town. A pedestrian archway through the bar was constructed in the 1860s, and the bar is now a major tourist attraction, being the last example of the town's ancient defences.

This view of around 1910 showing North Bar Without provides an example of the interesting clusters of varied architecture that appear throughout Beverley. To the right is Bar House, an eighteenth-century house restyled in 1866; in the centre the North Bar, and to its left a terrace of Georgian houses, the last of which has been rebuilt and adapted to form part of the corner buildings. This work was done for and partly by the woodcarver J.E. Elwell in the 1894-95, whose carvings adorn the mock half-timbered exterior. Beyond this is a small passage named Wylie's Yard that was opened out around 1959 to create Wylie's Road, which now links North Bar Without and Norwood. The new road was named after Robert Wylie J.P. whose house, shown far left, was demolished for its construction. Rather sadly, the ornate corner property now houses a pizza parlour amongst other things; a sign of changing modern habits, where more frequently we now choose to eat out.

A rather gloomy Hengate is shown here in October 1905 as crowds awaited the procession of King Edward VII, who was visiting the town. The origin of the name Hengate is unknown, but may hark back to the time when Saturday Market extended this far north; game and poultry may have been sold at this end of the market, hence Hen-Gate. Hengate leads eastwards from North Bar Within, to the former site of the Norwood Bar and on to Norwood itself. Possibly its most famous building is the White Horse Inn, probably Beverley's most complete old pub, dating from the seventeenth century, if not earlier. Hengate is relatively unchanged, except for the continual stream of traffic along its one-way system, and retains most of its old buildings. A noticeable exception is St Mary's House, shown in the centre of the earlier photograph, which was destroyed in a fire in 1912 and never rebuilt. The site was donated to the town in 1917 and now forms part of the memorial gardens.

Ladygate, known as St Mary Gate in the thirteenth century, was literally, the way to St Mary's church. The twelfth century church has seen little change, whereas Ladygate is very much changed in places. Originally, Ladygate only stretched from Hengate as far as Sow Hill, and the north end of the Market Place. Gradually, during the seventeenth and

eighteenth centuries, new blocks of property were built filling the north-east corner of the market; effectively extending Ladygate further south.

A new road, named Sow Hill Road, was cut through from Walkergate to the north of the Market around 1968; this forced the demolition of one of Beverley's oldest and most historic inns. The Globe Inn, dating from the seventeenth century, can be seen centre left of this photograph taken around 1908; it was swept away for a road that Beverley could easily have done without.

Thankfully, many original properties in this photograph have survived, and are now used for a variety of trades including cafes and a kitchen utensil shop.

Walkergate, first recorded as early as 1329, took its name from the many walkers or fullers in the cloth manufactories; materials were processed by walking on the cloth (possibly in the nearby Walker Beck) during the process of fulling, to condense the fibres of the material.

Modern traffic levels caused demolition of parts of the ancient road, as the Walkergate Relief Road was planned from the late 1960s; construction of New Walkergate was completed 1979-80, although not officially named until 1985. The east, or right side of this picture survives with the loss of just one house, whereas the west side no longer exists, and is the site of the northbound lanes of the new road.

The tall building in the distance was the 'public rooms', built around 1840, behind the ballroom of the Assembly Rooms of 1762. The rooms were converted to form the Regal Cinema in 1935, which was recently demolished and is the site of housing, offices and a restaurant.

Norwood forms a very old alignment, and once led to a long-forgotten woodland area known as the North Wood, hence the name; first recorded as 'Norwode' in 1308, then 'North Wood,' eventually corrupted to the present Norwood from the fifteenth century.

The shop of Rhoda Hunsley, shown on page 32, can just be seen to the extreme left of this picture showing the south-west side of Norwood around 1905. To the extreme right of the picture is the butcher's shop of Phineas Musgrave, who was landlord of the Valiant Soldier pub next door, now known as the Cornerhouse. Almost all of the property from the pub eastwards has now been demolished; No. 14 survives, dating from the eighteenth century it is now a music shop. Also surviving is the butchers, which remains one of Beverley's few independent butchers.
The building with the overhanging porch, in the centre of the photograph, was known as the Old Porch House and was probably sixteenth century.

As Norwood was built up with housing, from the end of the nineteenth century, many of the old shops and businesses were lost. This photograph taken around 1907, shows the line of property that continued from the left side of the last photograph. On the right is the house of builder and contractor Richard Potts, who may well have carried out some of the building work. Beyond his premises is a long terrace, often referred to as Norwood Walk; this was foreshortened by three properties in 1937 to create the entrance to Corporation Road. This turned the old Durham Ox pub into a corner property, which it remains today. Just a few doors east of the pub was another, known as the Gate; its hanging sign can be seen in the photograph. Sadly modern flats now occupy the site of Norwood Walk, as modern housing replaced the old property, which was no doubt declared unfit.

The hamlet of Grovehill or 'Gruvale', first mentioned around 1156, was formed around a riverside berth at the River Hull, where goods were unloaded for road transport to Beverley before the Beck came into use. Later recorded as 'Groval' or 'Grovel', Grovehill Road has developed from the old trade route from the hamlet to Beverley centre, into a long suburban street, which has sadly become very industrialised at its eastern end. Victorian shipyards and mills have lead to the area being used by many small firms, whose works now cover the ancient site.

Fortunately, as can be seen from the two photographs, the intervening years have brought less change. The 2006 view, when compared to the older photograph of around 1905, shows only the two small blocks of houses in the centre have been lost. Encouragingly, small housing developments have been constructed in recent years, to the rear of these older properties, on the north side of the street.

In the centre of this photograph taken around 1910, is the former Nag's Head pub, which served the locals of Grovehill and Weel from the eighteenth century until its closure around 1910. The Nag's Head, as with many pubs located at the site of a ferry, had also served as the home of the ferryman and his family. In the foreground is the old floating pontoon swing bridge, which replaced a ramshackle ferry boat that had been located here since the fifteenth century; this linked Beverley with the tiny, and ancient, township of Weel on the east bank. The floating bridge system, opened in 1884, remained in use until 1949, when it sank and a small boat was again used; this too was made redundant, when the present toll-free Weel Bridge was constructed further south in 1953.

The modern view shows how the nature of this thriving ship-building, milling and nautical area has all but disappeared; only small remnants of the shipyard remain but nothing from the earlier view.

6

Trade and Industry

The extensive works shown in this photograph taken around 1905 can be seen in the background of the picture on the previous page; this was Crathorne & Sons flour mill at Grovehill, viewed from the bridge over the Beverley and Barmston drain.

Two windmills were situated at Grovehill at the beginning of the nineteenth century, one of which was purchased by Josiah and Robert Crathorne in 1830, to mill flour and grain. Following a fire in 1858 the mill was converted for steam as well as wind power; this, and the ability to obtain imported grain via the river, gave Crathorne's a major advantage and by 1900 theirs was the only working mill left in Beverley. In January 1907 another fire occurred and the mill closed, probably due to a market that by then was dominated by the mills in Hull. Minimal fire fighting is shown in this 1912 photograph, which recorded the event.

In 2006 there is no trace of the former mill, only small industrial units now line the banks of the drain. The Crathorne's name lives on in Beverley; Crathorne's Cottages, built for mill workers, still exist on the north side of Grovehill Road, and in 1947 a new road between Hodgson Avenue and Coltman Avenue was named Crathorne Avenue.

The name of Straker had been well known in Beverley, as the Straker family had been brewers and innkeepers in the town for generations. From the late 1880s Robert Biglin Straker operated as the East Riding Mineral Water Co. (later The East Riding Aerated Water Works), from premises at No. 81 Walkergate, shown in this trade advertisement from around 1913. Thomas G. Straker had taken over the business in the late 1890s, when Robert moved to set up business in Hull. Later operating simply as T.G. Straker Ltd, the firm continued trading in Beverley until the late 1950s.

As the growth of the supermarket and larger stores took hold, small businesses such as these were forced out of business; their main custom, probably being public houses, was also taken from them as the brewing giants took over and produced their own beverages or had national suppliers. The buildings shown have since been demolished, and the site partially built upon; latterly this was a carpet shop, but is now vacant and up for sale.

ADMIRAL TOGO.

The photographs shown here depict the shipbuilding industry, which had been located at Grovehill, on the banks of the River Hull, since the early eighteenth century at least. Top left on page 72 is a view of around 1904 showing Edwardians awaiting a ship launch; bottom left shows the launch of *Admiral Togo* on 13 August 1904, viewed from the east bank (note Crathorne's mill and the roof of the Nag's Head pub behind the vessel); on this page is a photograph taken in around 1920 looking north from the site of the present bridge (note the floating pontoon bridge in the distance), and a similar modern view. Ships as large as 1,500 tons were built in the yards, and the firm of Cochrane's built 245 vessels between 1884 and 1901, however shipbuilding ceased at Grovehill in 1979; only fragments of machinery remain from one of Beverley's greatest industries. Thankfully, the various boats moored by enthusiasts serve as some reminder of its former use.

It is not well known that motor cars were built in Beverley as early as 1909. Engineer Gordon Armstrong set up business in 1907 from an ancient timber-framed building in North Bar Within (see page 58). From his East Riding Engineering Works in Tiger Lane, he produced the Gordon car from 1909 until the First World War. The firm gained a reputation for quality shock absorbers, which made it a major name in that business, later operating from other sites as Armstrong Patents Ltd. Mr Armstrong, with hat and moustache, can be seen at the rear of the car chassis, in this photograph taken around 1910. A nine horsepower, water-cooled Gordon cost £135, an air-cooled model £125 and a four-seater was £165. The car could reach forty-five miles per hour and fuel consumption of fifty miles per gallon was advertised. The workshops in which Armstrong produced the car are now gone and his garage and offices are the site of a shopping arcade, as shown in the modern photograph.

This rather crowded joiner's shop was situated in Wood Lane, and probably that of carpenter and joiner Edwin Calvert. Dating from around 1910, it is interesting to see how even whilst at work, men at that time wore collar and tie. Most working class people would have very few outfits, unlike today when we buy clothes as a pastime or for fashionable reasons; in the Victorian and Edwardian era few could afford such luxury and men generally had two suits, one for work and one for everything other than work! In 2006 Beverley's main industries, engineering, tanning, shipbuilding, chemical manufacture, flour and grain milling and seed crushing, have all but gone and tourism is now a major hope for Beverley's future. Tourism is dependent on local attractions and shops; one area that attracts tourists as well as locals is antiques and collectibles, as supplied by dealers such as Chris Fowler from his arcade in Beverley; Chris is seen here outside The St Crispin's Antique Centre in Butcher Row.

Watts Bros was a familiar logo, emblazoned on the side of many a vehicle, once delivering goods around Beverley and Yorkshire. The firm of Watts Brothers began in the 1880s when John Watts was listed as a hay dealer etc in Lairgate. By 1892 he advertised a daily run to Hull and back as a carrier; in 1905 his wagon 'leaves Lairgate daily at 8 a. m., returning from the Rampant Horse Mytongate Hull at 3 p. m.' From around 1920 the firm became Watts Bros, operating from No. 49 Lairgate, shown in this photograph from around that time.

From the 1940s they offered house removals, car-hire, and road haulage throughout the country, and later had premises in Hull and Beverley. Latterly, their Lairgate depot in Beverley was used as a carpet warehouse; this was demolished in the winter of 2005/06 and the site has already been rebuilt with housing.

The effect of the railway on Beverley's trade and industry has been minimal. Beverley had been isolated prior to its arrival in 1846, except from Hull, where water and road links had been established for centuries. The railway arrived in Beverley just as the railway boom ended, causing links to other areas were delayed for twenty years. Trade may even have suffered due to its arrival; Crosskill's Ironworks exported goods via Hull, and no doubt lost business as customers could obtain goods from all over England as the railway came to Hull in 1840. Some shortlived benefits were seen, including the construction of the railway and its associated buildings, and the footbridge shown in this photograph taken around 1911. Crossing from Chantry Lane, west into Friars Lane, involved passing over the lines and for reasons of safety an overhead footbridge was constructed. The wooden bridge shown in the older photograph was later replaced by the present iron structure.

The name of Cherry was another well-known in Beverley; the family were millwrights and engineers in the town for over seventy years. The firm were established around 1890, and by 1892 Robert Foster Cherry was proudly advertising as millwright and engineer to (tanners) R. Hodgson & Sons, from his Queensgate address. By 1899 the Queensgate address was dealing with the cycle and motor car trade, whilst the engineering had moved to works at Beckside north. They later had a shop at No. 29 Eastgate, a cycle manufactory in North Bar Within and engineering works at No. 76 Lairgate.

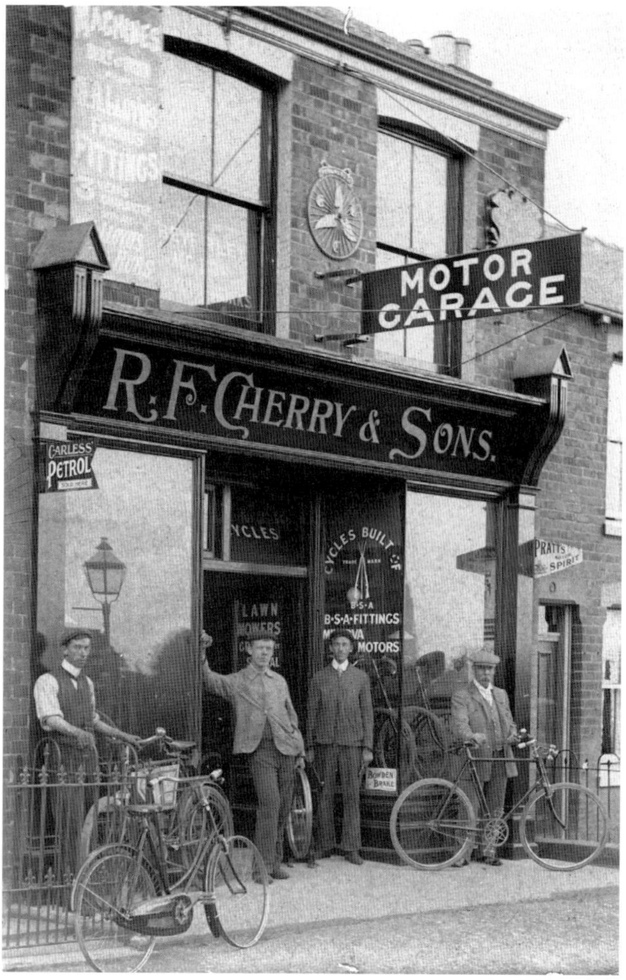

The garage at Nos 28-30 Queensgate lasted until the 1960s, and latterly the firm also ran Cherry's Coaches from this address and later in Walkergate. East Yorkshire Motor Services took over Cherry's Coaches on 13 April 1987 and drew the end to an era.

This photograph, taken around 1905, shows the Beverley Cycle Works at Queensgate Road, where they advertised as 'cycle and motor car agents', and 'manufacturers of the celebrated Beaver cycles.' The pair of buildings survive as a private house; the only evidence of its past use is a patch on the wall where the cycle club sign used to hang, and the frontage has been replaced with a car porch.

7

Suburbs and Side Streets

The north side of Norwood has changed little at this point; a pony and trap travels east, past the former Primitive Methodist Mission Room, on empty roads with no parked cars in this photograph taken around 1905.

As Beverley's population grew during the nineteenth century, new housing was required; to the east of the town, old religious sites and watercourses often restricted new development. Wilbert Lane is a very old alignment, first recorded as Oswaldgate in 1329 and later Hayrer or Hair Lane; many other names have been used but it has been recorded as Wilbert Lane since around 1820 at least. It may have taken its name from an ex-mayor of Beverley, Edward Wilbert. Buildings belonging to Crosskill's Beverley Iron & Waggon Co. Ltd can be seen in the distance in this photograph taken around 1905, and its workers were no doubt part of the demand for housing. The mostly Victorian houses, shown on both sides of the street, survive, but may now be inhabited by people who commute to work, rather than work locally. Where children played in empty streets, traffic now rules, and Wilbert Lane is a busy cut-through at peak times.

Like so many small towns, Beverley was once almost surrounded by orchards and market gardens, where fruit and vegetables were grown for trade and to feed the local population. The area around Wilbert Lane was filled with nurseries, but as housing demand grew, these were built over. Wilbert Grove was laid-out, extending south from Wilbert Lane around 1860 on the line of a footpath around the orchards and nurseries of Thomas Swailes' Providence Nursery. The street and houses were designed by Edward and Gregory Page, and mostly built by builder Robert Pape; the street is not shown on the 1851/54 Ordnance Survey plans of Beverley, and was not occupied until many years later.

The houses are of various dates as shown in this photograph of around 1905, and the scene is relatively unchanged in 2006, except once again the street is now crowded with parked and moving cars.

Woodlands is still arguably made up of two older streets, divided by a line of trees shown in these photographs; Love Lane, a narrow street on the south leading to the Westwood, first known as Balme Close Lane or Narrow Lane; and Union Road to the north, constructed in 1861 as a road to the Union Workhouse (see page 41) which opened that year. Housing appeared on the north side of the street when Alexandra Terrace was built by builder Thomas Dalton and joiner Richard Farrah in 1863; the present name comes from a block of property constructed on the south side (Love Lane) in the 1890s, called Woodlands, as it backed onto a large wood, north of Westwood Lane.

The division of the two streets has merged; note how Love Lane was blocked on the left with two posts in the photograph taken *c.*1920. Woodlands has two cul-de-sacs on its north side; Quaker Lane (built around 1968) and Woodlands Drive (built around 1960), and is a very desirable area.

Wood Lane's name reflects its close proximity to the Westwood, once filled with trees, and a smaller wood that lay between Woodlands and Westwood Road. It is likely that the alignment of Wood Lane formed part of an ancient route through Beverley leading from Holderness and the east via Norwood, Hengate, Wood Lane and west over the pastures to Cave and Howden.

It is recorded as early as 1416, as Wode Lane, and its older eastern end was also known as Tongs Lane. The eastern end, nearest North Bar Within, was home to many small businesses, and Wood Lane also had its own small pub – the Blue Bell Inn; the inn was recorded from the 1860s and closed in the 1954, but the building survives. These days Wood Lane is still a very attractive street and most of the buildings from the older photograph survive; even the old lamppost has remained unchanged, and the only new buildings are at the east end.

Denton Street forms part of a suburban development of predominantly working class housing to the east of the town around Holme Church Lane, built in the early years of the last century. Denton Street itself was built around 1904 on land belonging to the Denton family, who were major landowners in the Beverley area, and also had interests in the tanning industry.

The smart, regimented appearance of the street shown in the photograph of around 1908 has been lost, as shown by many of the modern photographs in this book. The fashion to modernise and improve our homes has given many of us our own unique look, but has left an untidy feeling to many streets. The loss of the iron railings during the Second World War may have begun the change, and during the 1960s it was the fashion to throw out all that was old. Ironically, many of us are now replacing the original features in our homes and many streets are returning to their original appearance.

Another street affected by the Holme Church Lane development was Beaver Road, located almost opposite Denton Street shown on page 84. An old alignment, the street had been known as Bogle Lane, Boggle Lane and Bog Hill Lane from the 1840s and ran through the site of many nurseries and market gardens; thankfully, following protests from the residents, the street acquired a new title. The present name was approved in 1903, taking its inspiration from the humble Beaver, which forms part of the insignia and town crest of Beverley.

The housing in the street is mostly Victorian, and once again has become a bit of a hotchpotch of design and taste. Again, the modern requirement for at least one car per household has caused the street to become less of a playground, as shown in the photograph dated around 1905, and more of a car park.

Beverley is a town of many pubs, some of which have served their local community for hundreds of years. Beverley's suburbs and side streets hide little gems; one of which is the Woolpack Inn, in Westwood Road. Built in the 1820s it became a pub in 1837 and later had a small brewhouse and stabling for three horses. The Hull Brewery Co. Ltd leased the pub from 1896, and bought it outright in 1936, which is probably the date of this photograph. The Woolpack is a Listed Building, but has sadly lost some of its original features; the marvellous hanging bracket and globe lamp have gone, as has the flag pole attached to the chimney stack. Fortunately, it has survived most attempts to modernise it and is a pleasant retreat for the locals, who regard it very much their own.

As new housing developments stretched out around Beverley and the suburbs grew, they created a demand for new facilities; families had little means of transport and new shops, churches, pubs and schools had to be built locally to serve the new population. Housing in Norwood spread steadily further east, creating its own suburban population, and in 1875 St Mary's National School for girls was built on the north side of the road. Designed by J.B. and W. Atkinson of York, the school was built in the Gothic style and average attendance was 200-250 pupils. In 1970 the school amalgamated with the boys' school and was taken over by nearby Beverley High School for girls in 1975.

These days, schools are a different affair, and places are sought at the best schools, causing pupils to travel far and wide to school on buses or in their parents' cars, adding to Beverley's traffic woes. The style of dress has also changed, with pupils now able to express a certain amount of independence.

As the main road frontages became fully built upon, smaller side streets were developed running off. One such street was Norwood Grove, which runs off the north side of Norwood. Seen here around 1905, the street was originally developed around 1860, initially as a cul-de-sac. Following the construction of Laughton Road in 1970/71, Norwood Grove became an access road to Laughton Road, and links with Norwood Far Grove. This has caused the now familiar problem of traffic congestion, and a street that was once a quiet backwater has become rather overcrowded. Fortunately, most of the original property remains intact and residents do what they can to preserve the integrity of the street.

The former Dominican friary, mentioned on page 46, gave rise to a number of street names in the surrounding area. Thus Friars Lane, Chantry Lane and this street Priory Road were named, as they stood on or around the site of the historic buildings. The street is in effect an extension of Chantry Lane, and follows the line of an ancient footpath that linked the friary with Grovehill Lane, shown on the 1854 Ordnance Survey plans of the area. The open land that the footpath crossed was gradually used for nurseries, and later was the site of tanneries. As the suburban side streets developed, the nurseries were built over and Priory Road was used for housing, inhabited from the latter years of the nineteenth century. The street looks remarkably unchanged in 2006, and the only noticeable difference is the loss of the iron railings, the ever-present parked cars and modern double-glazing.

Beverley Barracks.

Beverley had only a minimal military presence in the eighteenth century, and it was not until the East Riding Militia was formed in 1808, that permanent premises were sought. The first small sites were in the Guildhall, Waltham Lane, and from 1853 at a purpose-built barracks in New Walk. The demand for housing land had grown within the town, and the militia were forced into site out of town. This building was used until 1878, but a larger site had already been acquired in 1874, near Queensgate, and a new barracks was built, completed in 1877. These became known as the Victoria Barracks, and remained in use until 1961; the site was sold in 1977, and the barracks were demolished in 1982. The site is now partly a retail park, and partly modern housing. The supermarket chain of Morrison's opened one of their stores here on 4 February 1992, which now occupies the site of the buildings shown in these photographs dated around 1910. It is hard to imagine the barracks site now, but they are remembered in displays within the supermarket, and the architects of the supermarket have attempted some similarity with the lost buildings.

Lord Roberts Road was officially opened in 1909, as shown in this photograph, which shows the official parade with crowds waiting in the distance to walk on the new tarmac. Lord Frederick Roberts was noted in the South African War, and died in 1914. The new road linked Wednesday Market with Well Lane and Champney Road (then known as Captain Lane), forming a more direct route from the railway station to Lairgate. The view today is much changed; the back of the property on Highgate, to the right, is now obscured by trees. The hoardings to the right in the old photograph, mark a plot acquired for a 'new Baptist church', which opened in 1910 and is today used by Beverley Archives and as the Beverley studio of the BBC Radio Humberside. Just behind the photographer is a major new development in the area, council offices, and the site for Beverley's new six million pound heritage centre, to be known as the Treasure House.

Beverley has sadly lost some fine houses over the years; this was a typical example, known as Albion House. Situated on the south side of Grovehill Lane, nearest the Swinemoor roundabout. It was a very unusual house, possibly unique in Beverley, with Dutch gables and many other interesting architectural features. Many of Beverley's merchants and business men built themselves grand houses as a sign of their wealth, and fortunately many survive; Beverley became a place not just to set up business, but to retire to in the nineteenth century, which explains the huge amount of housing in its suburbs and side streets. Albion House was the home of John Charles Barker, of the seed-crushing firm Sheardown & Barker, from around 1892, which is probably the date it was constructed. Sadly, after falling into disuse it was demolished in 1985 and a cul-de-sac of new housing built on its site, named as Albion Court in 1986.

Longcroft Hall is actually situated in a small township one mile north of Beverley, known as Molescroft. Molescroft grew rapidly during the 1920s and is now effectively a suburb of Beverley, with no distinguishable boundary. Several large Victorian and Edwardian houses were built off the main road, such as this one known as Longcroft Hall; built around 1863, to the designs of architect William Botterill, and constructed by J.A. Hudson, the son of a Hull brick maker. Engineer Gordon Armstrong (see page 74) lived at the grand house, situated at the end of Gallows Lane, during the 1930s and 1940s. The house and some of its grounds were later used for the site of a school and technical college, which has involved quite drastic alteration of the house over the years. It is now part of the East Riding College of Beverley, and a new school was built in 1949, this later amalgamated with Molescroft County Secondary School in 1960 to form Longcroft School. This was enlarged with a new building in 1973, increasing the accommodation 1,700 pupils.

In the background of this peaceful view of around 1905, can be seen the north side of Woodlands (see page 82), and leading up to it is St Mary's Terrace, with Westwood Road leading off to the left. Its name was chosen as it stands on lands belonging to St Mary's church. It forms part of an extremely attractive area, which has become one of the most desirable in Beverley, and quite rightly so; its houses have mostly retained their character, and residents take great care to keep original details and preserve the streetscape as it once was. St Mary's and the streets adjoining are an excellent example of how Beverley has almost survived change from 'then until now'.

Other local titles published by Tempus

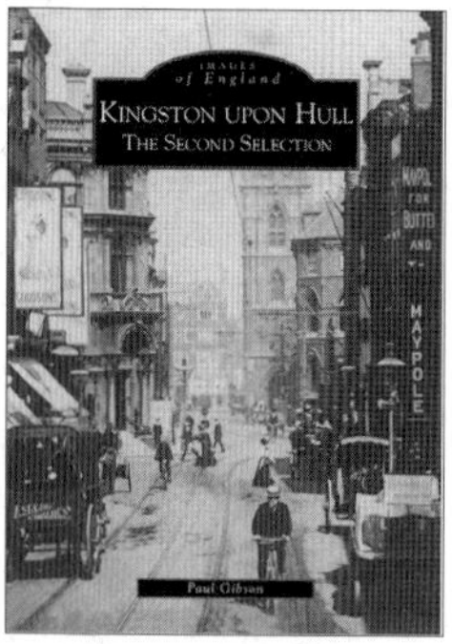

Kingston upon Hull – The Second Selection

PAUL GIBSON

Kingston upon Hull is a city of great variety and contrast, including docks, industry, civic buildings and residential areas. This selection of archive images brings to life many of the streets and long-forgotten work places which have disappeared or have changed beyond recognition. This book offers many nostalgic memories for those who remember how the city used to be.

0 7524 2607 9

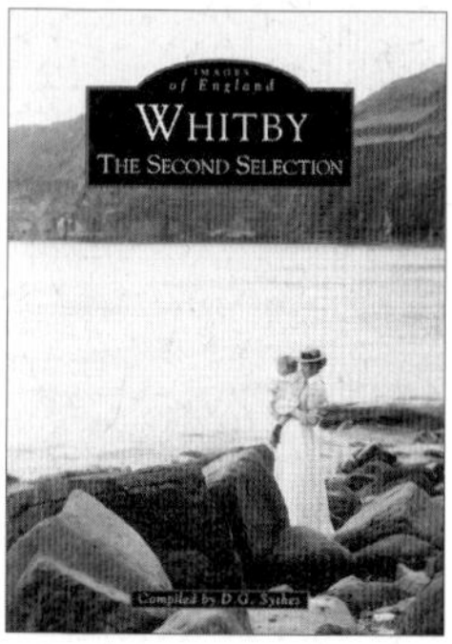

Whitby – The Second Selection

D.G. SYTHES

With over 200 fascinating images, never or rarely seen in print before, Des Sythes looks at the people who made the Whitby community what it is today. The work of many notable photographers such as Frank Sutcliffe, Hugh Lambert-Smith and Tom Watson is included within this selection of pictures, which makes this book visually absorbing, as well as excellently well-written.

0 7524 1610 3

Filey

PETER HARRIS

Filey has been a popular holiday destination for over a century. This splendid collection of more than 200 photographs, including many taken by the Victorian photographer Walter Fisher (who travelled around the district in a horse-drawn cart), explores the changing requirements of tourists over the decades. The author's life-time love of the resort has encouraged him to research and publish this nostalgic tribute.

0 7524 3847 6

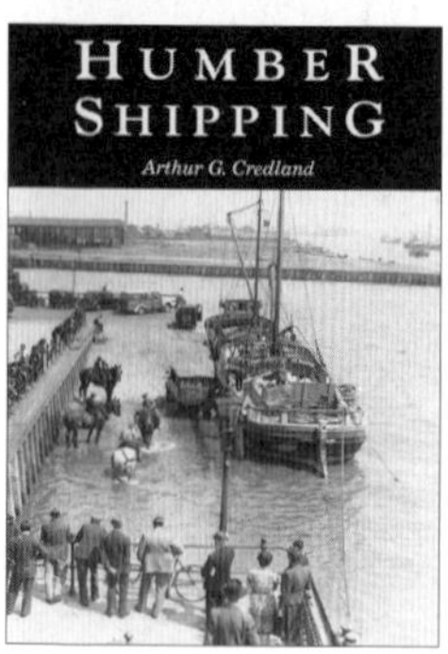

Humber Shipping

ARTHUR G. CREDLAND

Kingston upon Hull has been a major port since medieval times, and over a long period the city grew to be one of Britain's major ports and shipbuilding centres. Today the Humber looks much different than it did even ten years ago. Many docks and warehouses have gone and the fishing fleet is greatly reduced. Illustrated with over 200 images *Humber Shipping* reveals the changing face of the Humber's maritime history.

0 7524 2358 4

If you are interested in purchasing other books published by Tempus, or in case you have difficulty finding any Tempus books in your local bookshop, you can also place orders directly through our website

www.tempus-publishing.com